Ten P
from S

Candlestick Press

Published by:
Candlestick Press,
Diversity House, 72 Nottingham Road, Arnold, Nottingham UK NG5 6LF
www.candlestickpress.co.uk

Design and typesetting by Diversity Creative Marketing Solutions Ltd.,
www.diversity.agency

Printed by Ratcliff & Roper Print Group, Nottinghamshire, UK

Introduction and selection © Don Paterson, 2018

Cover illustration © Iain McIntosh, 2014
www.iainmcintosh.com

Candlestick Press monogram © Barbara Shaw, 2008

© Candlestick Press, 2014
Reprinted 2022.

First published 2014
Second edition, revised 2018

ISBN 978 1 907598 68 5

Acknowledgements:

The poems in this pamphlet are reprinted from the following books, all by permission of the publishers listed unless stated otherwise. Every effort has been made to trace the copyright holders of the poems published in this book. The editor and publisher apologise if any material has been included without permission or without the appropriate acknowledgement, and would be glad to be told of anyone who has not been consulted. Thanks are due to all the copyright holders cited below for their kind permission:

Jason Watts for permission to reprint 'Mouse skeleton', commended in the 2002 National Poetry Competition and published first in *Magma (No.25, Winter 2003)* and also in *Their Proper Names* (Stone Pig Press, 2007). Veronica Forrest-Thomson, 'Phrase-Book' is from Veronica Forrest-Thomson, *Collected Poems*, ed. Anthony Barnett (Shearsman Books, in assoc. with Allardyce Book, 2008), Copyright © Jonathan Culler and The Estate of Veronica Forrest-Thomson, 2008. Our thanks for permission to reproduce 'Etching of a Line of Trees' © John Glenday, 2009 (from *Grain*, Picador, 2009) and 'The Graduates' © Kathleen Jamie, 1999 (from *Jizzen*, Picador, 1999). 'Empty Vessel' by Hugh MacDiarmid is reprinted from *Complete Poems, Volume One* (Carcanet Press, 1993). WS Graham, 'Loch Thom', from *New Collected Poems* (Faber and Faber, 2005) is reproduced by kind permission of Rosalind Mudaliar. 'Re-reading Katherine Mansfield's *Bliss and Other Stories*' by Douglas Dunn is reprinted by permission of United Agents on behalf of Douglas Dunn. Jackie Kay 'Brendon Gallacher' from *Darling, New & Selected Poems* (Bloodaxe Books, 2007) by permission of the publisher. Edwin Morgan 'From the Video Box, 25' from *New Selected Poems* (Carcanet Press, 2000).

Where poets are no longer living, their dates are given.

Contents

		Page
Introduction	*Don Paterson*	5
Mouse skeleton	*Jason Watts*	7
Re-reading Katherine Mansfield's *Bliss and Other Stories*	*Douglas Dunn*	8
Etching of a Line of Trees	*John Glenday*	9
From the Video Box, 25	*Edwin Morgan*	*10 – 11*
The Graduates	*Kathleen Jamie*	*12*
Brendon Gallacher	*Jackie Kay*	*13*
Loch Thom	*WS Graham*	*14 – 15*
Phrase-Book	*Veronica Forrest-Thomson*	*16*
Address to the Unco Guid, or the Rigidly Righteous	*Robert Burns*	*17 – 19*
Empty Vessel	*Hugh MacDiarmid*	*20*

Introduction

Impossible tasks can tell you a great deal about yourself. When Candlestick Press asked me to choose just ten Scottish poems for this chapbook, I was immediately forced to distinguish between poems I loved rather than (as it turned out) merely admired. These are, of course, not all the Scottish poems I love. I realise I've stuck almost exclusively to 20th century or near-contemporary poets, but please don't assume this means I don't love the Makars: I just don't think their strong flavour works best in what's intended as a representative spoonful of a whole poetry. It probably does indicate an indifference for most things in Scottish poetry – excepting Burns and Fergusson – until we get to MacDiarmid. But right now all I see are my beloved omissions: favourite poems by Soutar, MacCaig, Crichton Smith, Maclean, Lochhead, Crawford, Burnside... Poems I'd love to have included, given the luxury of twenty choices.

So it's an indefensibly capricious selection, and one that probably reveals as much about how I feel about Scotland as its verse. 'Scotland' isn't a literary boundary, it's a political one. Up here we write in English, almost exclusively – and most writers consider their language the more important of their nationalities; most of my own favourite poets are Irish or American. For that reason, I suspect this little selection says as much about what I think about 'Scottishness' as Scottish poetry. Directly or indirectly, most of the poems here address just that.

Several of these poems reflect the national obsession with exile – even if it's the kind of internal exile from one's own class and language that Kathleen Jamie describes in 'The Graduates'.

Others demonstrate what I think of as a Scottish flair for bold experiment, whether it's WS Graham's unique take on English syntax in his heartbreaking 'Loch Thom', or Veronica Forrest-Thomson's brilliant deconstruction of the communication model in poems like 'Phrase-Book'. We also excel, I think, at the anti-baroque: leaving words standing so sharp and stark and bold on the page that you can hear the wind whistle round them. This ability to make each phrase a discrete lyric event I hear in poems by Jason Watts and Douglas Dunn.

If I'd been asked to choose just one poem, it would probably have been MacDiarmid's devastating 'Empty Vessel'. This is a touchstone poem for me, and reminds me what poetry can do to the human heart when it has the nerve, skill and ambition. That the poem is in Scots I find the least interesting thing about it. All these are poems are very 'Scottish' in a sense I immediately recognise, and show aspects of our literary character I think admirable and distinct. I hope this wee buik will serve as a prompt to explore our poetry further.

Don Paterson

Mouse skeleton

So quietly, decorously
in the tide of dust,
the moment of grace
untied what you so nervously

embodied. Unbodied solo
under festoons of webs,
among stoor and heads
of wasps, and their burst bike's halo.

You left just your inner shell,
a rack of suggestion,
delicate pedestal
on which to set this world running pell-mell.

Jason Watts

Re-reading Katherine Mansfield's *Bliss and Other Stories*

A pressed fly, like a skeleton of gauze,
Has waited here between page 98
And 99, in the story called "Bliss",
Since the summer of '62, its date,

Its last day in a trap of pages. Prose
Fly, what can "Je ne parle pas français" mean
To you who died in Scotland, when I closed
These two sweet pages you were crushed between?

Here is a green bus ticket for a week
In May, my place mark in "The Dill Pickle".
I did not come home that Friday. I flick
Through all our years, my love, and I love you still.

These stories must have been inside my head
That day, falling in love, preparing this
Good life; and this, this fly, verbosely buried
In "Bliss", one dry tear punctuating "Bliss".

Douglas Dunn

Etching of a Line of Trees

i.m. John Goodfellow Glenday

I carved out the careful absence of a hill and a hill grew.
I cut away the fabric of the trees
and the trees stood shivering in the darkness.

When I had burned off the last syllables of wind,
a fresh wind rose and lingered.
But because I could not bring myself

to remove you from that hill,
you are no longer there. How wonderful it is
that neither of us managed to survive

when it was love that surely pulled the burr
and love that gnawed its own shape from the burnished air
and love that shaped that absent wind against a tree.

Some shadow's hands moved with my hands
and everything I touched was turned to darkness
and everything I could not touch was light.

John Glenday

From the Video Box

25

If you ask what my favourite programme is
it has to be that strange world jigsaw final.
After the winner had defeated all his rivals
with harder and harder jigsaws, he had to prove his mettle
by completing one last absolute mindcrusher
on his own, under the cameras, in less than a week.
We saw, but he did not, what the picture would be:
the mid-Atlantic, photographed from a plane,
as featureless a stretch as could be found,
no weeds, no flotsam, no birds, no oil, no ships,
the surface neither stormy nor calm, but ordinary,
a light wind on a slowly rolling swell.
Hand-cut by a fiendish jigger to simulate,
but not to have, identical beaks and bays,
it seemed impossible; but the candidate –
he said he was a stateless person, called himself Smith –
was impressive: small, dark, nimble, self-contained.
The thousands of little grey tortoises were scattered
on the floor of the studio; we saw the clock; he started.
His food was brought to him, but he hardly ate.
He had a bed, with the light only dimmed to a weird blue,
never out. By the first day he had established
the edges, saw the picture was three metres long
and appeared to represent (dear God!) the sea.
Well, it was a man's life, and the silence
(broken only by sighs, click of wood, plop of coffee
in paper cups) that kept me fascinated.
Even when one hand was picking the edge-pieces
I noticed his other hand was massing sets
of distinguishing ripples or darker cross-hatching or
incipient wave-crests; his mind,
if not his face, worked like a sea.

It was when he suddenly rose from his bed
at two, on the third night, went straight over
to one piece and slotted it into a growing central patch,
then back to bed, that I knew he would make it.
On the sixth day he looked haggard and slow,
with perhaps a hundred pieces left,
of the most dreary unmarked lifeless grey.
The camera showed the clock more frequently.
He roused himself, and in a quickening burst
of activity, with many false starts, began
to press that inhuman insolent remnant together.
He did it, on the evening of the sixth day.
People streamed onto the set. Bands played.
That was fine. But what I liked best
was the last shot of the completed sea,
filling the screen; then the saw-lines disappeared,
till almost imperceptibly the surface moved
and it was again the real Atlantic, glad
to distraction to be released, raised
above itself in growing gusts, allowed
to roar as rain drove down and darkened,
allowed to blot, for a moment, the orderer's hand.

Edwin Morgan (1920 – 2010)

The Graduates

If I chose children they'd know
stories of the old country, the place
we never left. I swear

I remember no ship
slipping from the dock,
no cluster of hurt, proud family

waving till they were wee
as china milkmaids
on a mantelpiece,

but we have surely gone,
and must knock
with brass kilted pipers

the doors to the old land:
we emigrants of no farewell
who keep our bit language

in jokes and quotes;
our working knowledge
of coal-pits, fevers, lost

like the silver bangle I lost
at the shows one Saturday,
tried to conceal, denied

but they're not daft.
And my bright, monoglot bairns
will discover, misplaced

among the bookshelves,
proof, rolled in a red tube:
my degrees, a furled sail, my visa.

Kathleen Jamie

Brendon Gallacher *(For my brother Maxie)*

He was seven and I was six, my Brendon Gallacher.
He was Irish and I was Scottish, my Brendon Gallacher.
His father was in prison; he was a cat burglar.
My father was a communist party full-time worker.
He had six brothers and I had one, my Brendon Gallacher.

He would hold my hand and take me by the river
Where we'd talk all about his family being poor.
He'd get his mum out of Glasgow when he got older.
A wee holiday someplace nice. Some place far.
I'd tell my mum about my Brendon Gallacher

How his mum drank and his daddy was a cat burglar.
And she'd say, 'why not have him round to dinner?'
No, no, I'd say he's got big holes in his trousers.
I like meeting him by the burn in the open air.
Then one day after we'd been friends two years,

One day when it was pouring and I was indoors,
My mum says to me, 'I was talking to Mrs Moir
Who lives next door to your Brendon Gallacher
Didn't you say his address was 24 Novar?
She says there are no Gallachers at 24 Novar

There never have been any Gallachers next door.'
And he died then, my Brendon Gallacher,
Flat out on my bedroom floor, his spiky hair,
His impish grin, his funny flapping ear.
Oh Brendon. Oh my Brendon Gallacher.

Jackie Kay

Loch Thom

                 1

Just for the sake of recovering
I walked backward from fifty-six
Quick years of age wanting to see,
And managed not to trip or stumble
To find Loch Thom and turned round
To see the stretch of my childhood
Before me. Here is the loch. The same
Long-beaked cry curls across
The heather-edges of the water held
Between the hills a boyhood's walk
Up from Greenock. It is the morning.

And I am here with my mammy's
Bramble jam scones in my pocket.
The Firth is miles and I have come
Back to find Loch Thom maybe
In this light does not recognise me.

This is a lonely freshwater loch.
No farms on the edge. Only
Heather grouse-moor stretching
Down to Greenock and One Hope
Street or stretching away across
Into the blue moors of Ayrshire.

2

And almost I am back again
Wading the heather down to the edge
To sit. The minnows go by in shoals
Like iron-filings in the shallows.

My mother is dead. My father is dead
And all the trout I used to know
Leaping from their sad rings are dead.

3

I drop my crumbs into the shallow
Weed for the minnows and pinheads.
You see that I will have to rise
And turn round and get back where
My running age will slow for a moment
To let me on. It is a colder
Stretch of water than I remember.

The curlew's cry travelling still
Kills me fairly. In front of me
The grouse flurry and settle. GOBACK
GOBACK GOBACK FAREWELL LOCH THOM.

WS Graham (1918 – 1986)

Phrase-Book

Words are a monstrous excrescence.
Everything green is extended. It
is apricot, orange, lemon, olive and cherry,
and other snakes in the linguistic grass;
also a white touch of marble which evokes
no ghosts, the taste of squid, the…
Go away. I shall call a policeman.
Acrocorinth which evokes no
goats under the lemon blossom.

World is a monstrous excrescence;
he is following me everywhere, one
Nescafé and twenty Athenes, everything
green; I am not responsible for it.
I don't want to speak to you.
Leave me alone. I shall stay here.
I refuse a green extension. Beware.
I have paid you. I have paid you
enough, sea, sun, and octopodi.
It is raining cats and allomorphs.

"Where" is the British Embassy.

Veronica Forrest-Thomson (1947 – 1975)

Address to the Unco Guid, or the Rigidly Righteous

My Son, these maxims make a rule,
  And lump them ay thegither;
The Rigid Righteous *is a fool,*
  The Rigid Wise *anither:*
The cleanest corn that e'er was dight
  May hae some pyles o' caff in;
So ne'er a fellow-creature slight
  For random fits o' daffin.
                    Solomon – Eccles. ch.vii. vers. 16.

I
O ye wha are sae guid yoursel,
  Sae pious and sae holy,
Ye've nought to do but mark and tell
  Your Neebours' fauts and folly!
Whase life is like a weel-gaun mill,
  Supply'd wi' store o' water,
The heaped happer's ebbing still,
  And still the clap plays clatter.

II
Hear me, ye venerable Core,
  As counsel for poor mortals,
That frequent pass douce Wisdom's door
  For glaikit Folly's portals;
I, for their thoughtless, careless sakes
  Would here propone defences,
Their donsie tricks, their black mistakes,
  Their failings and mischances.

III

Ye see your state wi' theirs compar'd,
   And shudder at the niffer,
But cast a moment's fair regard
   What maks the mighty differ;
Discount what scant occasion gave,
   That purity ye pride in,
And (what's aft mair than a' the lave)
   Your better art o' hiding.

IV

Think, when your castigated pulse
   Gies now and then a wallop,
What ragings must his veins convulse,
   That still eternal gallop:
Wi' wind and tide fair i' your tail,
   Right on ye scud your sea-way;
But, in the teeth o' baith to sail,
   It maks an unco leeway.

V

See Social-life and Glee sit down,
   All joyous and unthinking,
Till, quite transmugrify'd, they're grown
   Debauchery and Drinking:
O would they stay to calculate
   Th'eternal consequences;
Or your more dreaded h-ll to state,
   D-mnation of expences!

VI

Ye high, exalted, virtuous Dames,
   Ty'd up in godly laces,
Before ye gie poor *Frailty* names,
   Suppose a change o' cases;
A dear-lov'd lad, convenience snug,
   A treacherous inclination –
But, let me whisper i' your lug,
   Ye're aiblins nae temptation.

VII

Then gently scan your brother Man,
   Still gentler sister Woman;
Tho' they may gang a kennin wrang,
   To step aside is human:
One point must still be greatly dark,
   The moving *Why* they do it;
And just as lamely can ye mark,
   How far perhaps they rue it.

VIII

Who made the heart, 'tis *He* alone
   Decidedly can try us,
He knows each chord its various tone,
   Each spring its various bias:
Then at the balance let's be mute,
   We never can adjust it;
What's *done* we partly may compute,
   But know not what's *resisted*.

Robert Burns (1759 – 1796)

Empty Vessel

I met ayont the cairney
A lass wi' tousie hair
Singin' till a bairnie
That was nae langer there.

Wunds wi' warlds to swing
Dinna sing sae sweet,
The licht that bends owre a'thing
Is less ta'en up wi't.

Hugh MacDiarmid (1892 – 1978)